TICK ☑ TRACK 🐾 LISTEN ♫

Kruger

T0002162

HOW TO USE THIS BOOK

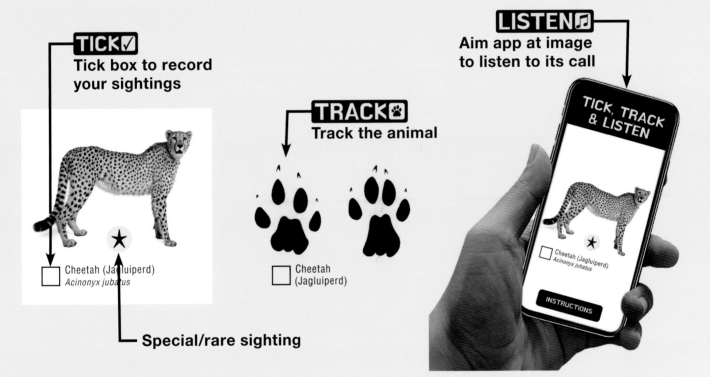

TICK ☑
Tick box to record your sightings

☐ Cheetah (Jagluiperd)
Acinonyx jubatus

★ → Special/rare sighting

TRACK 🐾
Track the animal

☐ Cheetah (Jagluiperd)

LISTEN ♫
Aim app at image to listen to its call

TICK, TRACK & LISTEN

☐ Cheetah (Jagluiperd)
Acinonyx jubatus

INSTRUCTIONS

HOW TO USE THE TICK, TRACK & LISTEN APP

Step 1: Point the camera on your phone at the QR code (or visit www.ticktrackandlisten.com).

Step 2: Click on the link.

Step 3: Download the app from the TICK, TRACK & LISTEN website.

Step 2: Open the app and point the phone at any species in the book.

Step 3: Listen to the sound of the animal.

MAMMALS

Most people go to the park to see animals. Some think only about sighting the Big Five – lion, leopard, elephant, buffalo and rhino. Others go there to hunt with their eyes and cameras, to see action and to marvel at the diversity. There is a lot to discover, and many information sources, but the most rewarding insights will be those you reach by yourself as you simply watch what animals do and try to understand why they do it.

When you come across animals, slow down and approach with caution. Be quiet and watch. Let things happen and be there to witness the action.

Animal numbers of the different species fluctuate all the time. For the species where a range of numbers is given, e.g. impala, the population estimate for these species is between the two numbers. These species are counted with a sample survey giving these ranges or confidence intervals.

GOOD TO KNOW

• The Kruger National Park is home to about **148 mammal species**.

• Mammals, like all other animals and plants, prefer certain habitats and can tolerate certain environmental conditions. Their preferences are basically determined by the kind of geology and weather of the region, because that in turn will determine the plants that may occur. Plant feeders differ in how specific their preferences are. Some will feed on a broad range of plant species, while others are partial to specific types. Carnivores follow plant feeders and are found wherever there are enough of them to prey on.

• Of all the mammals in the park, **78 species are small and not usually seen** on regular game drives. Of these, 42 are bat species; six shrews; three elephant shrews; two are golden moles; and 25 are rodent species.

• Of the rest, there are five primates; 27 carnivores; 23 bovids (including the buffalo and 22 antelopes); three rodents and 11 others.

• Of the **carnivores,** six are cats; four belong to the dog group; three are of the hyena group; eight are mongooses; and the others are the civet, genet, badger, otter and polecat.

• Mammals seen on the game drives include the **biggest** (elephant), the **tallest** (giraffe) and the **fastest** (cheetah) land mammals on Earth.

• **Early mornings** are good for **predator and scavenger** sightings, while **mid-mornings** are recommended for game **at drinking points**. During the **hot midday hours** most animals prefer to **rest and shelter** from the sun, and antelope use the time to ruminate. Animals that regularly **wallow** often do so when it is hot and muggy. These include buffalo, rhino, warthog and elephant.

• **Leopards** are basically nocturnal, but sightings are nevertheless reported throughout the day. They often rest on horizontal branches of marula, tamboti or jackalberry trees or in the deep shade of low shrubs where they blend perfectly with the dappled shadow patterns. It is estimated that there are about 2 000 leopards in the park.

• Surprisingly, there are fewer **lion** than leopard in the park, with numbers estimated at 1 750. They are also mainly nocturnal and most active in the early mornings and late afternoons. They spend 20 hours per day sleeping. Most lion kills are reported within two to three kilometres of their prey's drinking places.

• **Cheetah** are diurnal and can be encountered throughout the day. Their hunting technique requires open savanna where they can run down their prey. Since they are independent of water to a larger extent than other predators, they keep to drier areas where they can avoid competition from other predators. Sightings of these speedsters are special since their numbers are estimated at a mere 120 to 150 in the park.

• The extremely successful **spotted hyena** is an opportunist and mainly nocturnal. Their numbers are estimated at 5 340. Although regarded as prime scavengers, they actively hunt for most of their food. In Kruger they cover distances of up to 20 km in search of food but require regular access to water.

• **Wild dogs** are the most endangered of all predators. In the park they number between 150 and 300 and move and hunt in packs. They are most active during early morning or late afternoon and usually rest during the hottest part of the day. These dogs need lots of living space and prefer open savanna. It is difficult to predict where to find them.

Leopard Cubs

White Rhino

• Both **black-backed and side-striped jackal** are low-key predators in Kruger. Both are nocturnal but while the side-striped jackal is rarely seen, only at dawn or dusk or on heavily overcast days, the black-backed jackal is bolder during the day and often seen at carcasses or skulking around.

• **Caracal** sightings are rare, partly because they are nocturnal, but also because they are much smaller than the other predators and scavengers. Although they are widely distributed, look out for them in dry, rocky areas with adjacent plains.

• **Serval** are rarely seen on self-drives in Kruger since they are mainly active at dawn and dusk. They occur in wetland habitats where they hunt rodents and birds.

• The **African wild cat** is another rare sighting, but in Satara Camp there is often one wandering about scavenging at night. The very rare **black-footed cat** is occasionally seen on night drives in the Klopperfontein Dam area.

• **Smaller predators** such as the diurnal mongooses appear suddenly and are often gone before you can get a proper look. The slender mongoose with its long, black-tipped tail is always solitary; the banded mongooses move around in groups, usually close to rivers and trees; and the tiny dwarf mongooses use termite mounds as their castles and forage in surrounding grassland for insects.

• **Elephants** are distributed all over the park, but 60% occur in the north, 30% in the central parts and 10% in the south. They spend 18 to 19 hours per day feeding and are both nocturnal and diurnal. In most parts of Kruger they drink every day, preferring to do this in the late afternoon. The latest census estimated their numbers at 13 750.

• Look for **white rhino** in short grassland. They feed for at least 12 hours per day, and need shade, shelter and access to water and wallows. In summer, they may drink twice a day but usually prefer to drink in the late afternoon or early evening and wallow in the middle of the day. Most white rhino occur in the south of Kruger but their numbers have increased in the centre as they are slowly spreading north.

• **Black rhino** are extremely elusive and shy. Look deep into the bush and undergrowth. As browsers they prefer dense bush with tamboti as their favourite browse. Look for them in the dense Sabie/Crocodile river thorn thickets along the banks, but also further afield close to watercourses, since they drink regularly in the late evening or at night. The far side of Sunset Dam is a favourite drinking spot just before dusk.

• **Hippo** will be found along the major perennial rivers of the park. In the south they occur in the Crocodile and Sabie rivers; in the central area they may be found in the big perennial dams and deep pools such as Orpen Dam, Nsemani Dam, the N'wanetsi Dam and the Piet Grobler Dam in the Timbavati. Northwards, the Olifants River, and particularly the Letaba River, are home to big hippo pods. In the north, the Shingwedzi perennial pools and the Grootvlei Dam house a few, as do the deep perennial pools of the Luvuvhu and Limpopo rivers. Their present numbers are estimated at 3 100.

• Central Kruger ranging from the Sabie to the Olifants River is the hub for **giraffe**. Only 10% of the estimated population of 6 800–10 300 occur north of the Letaba River. They favour thorn trees such as umbrella thorn, knob-thorn, Delagoa thorn, horned thorn and others such as bushwillow and cluster-leaf. In the mopane veld, giraffe are mainly found along river courses where thorn trees grow.

- **Buffalo** are considered the most dangerous of all animals to hunt and are therefore included as one of the Big Five. Mixed herds (i.e. including males, females and young) numbering hundreds are often encountered on their way to drink. Being bulk grazers, they have to drink daily and sometimes even twice a day. There are probably in excess of 37 000 of these bovids in the park, of which more than 60% roam the northern parts where the biggest herds occur.

- **Plains zebra** are fussy when it comes to fresh drinking water, of which they require a regular supply. That is the driving force behind zebra migrations. When water supplies become inadequate, they move to find water and good grazing. The zebra migrations in the park are not as pronounced as those in the Serengeti, but north–south mini migrations do take place. The 30 000+ zebra are distributed all over the park but they always keep within 10 km of water.

- **Blue wildebeest** are often seen in close association with zebra. They do not compete for food as the zebra crop the taller grass and the wildebeest follow in their wake, as they like shorter pastures. About 6 400–13 100 or more of the estimated 15 000 individuals occur south of the Olifants River.

- **Impala** are prolific and occur from south to north in the park, but almost 80% occur south of the Olifants River. Their numbers are estimated at between 132 300 and 176 400.

- **Kudu** numbers in the park are estimated at 11 200–17 300. They are the second-tallest antelope, and have remarkable jumping abilities. They prefer thickets and browse a wide variety of plant species.

- **Nyala and bushbuck** are almost lookalikes. They occupy the same kind of habitat and feed on similar plant species. Nyala used to be confined to the Pafuri area but are now slowly spreading southwards along perennial rivers. There are only about 300 in the park.

- **Eland** are extremely rare in the park (estimated at 460), are seldom seen and very skittish.

- **Tsessebe** are also rare and skittish but are more often seen despite their low numbers (estimated at 180–220).

- The most beautiful and impressive antelope, the **sable**, is often seen in the Pretoriuskop area and north of N'watindlopfu on the H1-2 and along the S36. Numbers are estimated at 290.

- **Roan** numbers have diminished to such an extent that they are in danger of becoming extinct in the park. These antelope are seldom seen. Only between 90 individuals have been counted. Most sightings occur along the H1-7 and H1-8. There may still be a small population around Pretoriuskop.

- **Waterbuck** are favourite prey in certain parts of the park. They have increased in numbers over the years and estimations are that there may be 3 100-7 800 in the park.

- **Southern reedbuck** are scarce (about 300) since there are not many suitable habitats for them in Kruger.

- The **rarest antelope** is the **Lichtenstein's Hartebeest**, of which there are only a few left.

- **Steenbok** are prolific and so are **common duiker**. Oribi used to occur in the grasslands west of Pretoriuskop but have not been seen lately. **Mountain reedbuck** were reintroduced in the Berg-en-Dal area but probably did not survive. The occasional **suni** is seen around Punda Maria and **Sharpe's grysbok** are often encountered along riverine vegetation in the northern section of the park.

- **Primates** are usually found close to rivers or water points.

- Between 3 100 and 5 700 **warthogs** occur from south to north and are popular predator prey.

- **The best night-drive sightings** include lion, leopard, hyena, jackal, caracal, serval, wild cat, white-tailed mongoose, civet, pangolin, bushbaby (galago), genet, porcupine, spring hare, scrub hare and Cape hare. In regions where termite mounds are abundant, aardvark may be a very special sighting.

Hippopotamus and African Jacana

☐ Lion (Leeu)
Panthera leo

☐ Leopard (Luiperd)
Panthera pardus

☐ Cheetah (Jagluiperd)
Acinonyx jubatus

☐ Black-backed Jackal (Rooijakkals)
Canis mesomelas

☐ Side-striped Jackal (Witkwasjakkals)
Canus adustus

☐ African Wild Dog (Wildehond)
Lycaon pictus

☐ Spotted Hyena (Gevlekte Hiëna)
Crocuta crocuta

☐ Aardwolf (Aardwolf)
Proteles cristatus

☐ Caracal (Rooikat)
Caracal caracal

☐ African Wild Cat (Vaalboskat)
Felis lybica

☐ Serval (Tierboskat)
Leptailurus serval

☐ Honey Badger (Ratel)
Mellivora capensis

☐ Small-spotted Genet
(Kleinkolmuskejaatkat)
Genetta genetta

☐ Large-spotted Genet
(Grootkolmuskejaatkat)
Genetta tigrina

☐ African Civet (Siwetkat)
Civettictis civetta

☐ Banded Mongoose
(Gebande Muishond)
Mungos mungo

☐ Dwarf Mongoose
(Dwergmuishond)
Helogale parvula

☐ Slender Mongoose
(Swartkwasmuishond)
Galerella sanguinea

☐ White-tailed Mongoose
(Witstertmuishond)
Ichneumia albicauda

☐ African Savanna Elephant (Olifant)
Loxodonta africana

☐ White Rhinoceros (Witrenoster)
Ceratotherium simum

☐ Black Rhinoceros
(Swartrenoster)
Diceros bicornis

☐ Hippopotamus (Seekoei)
Hippopotamus amphibius

☐ African Buffalo (Buffel)
Syncerus caffer

☐ Giraffe (Kameelperd)
Giraffa camelopardalis

☐ Plains Zebra (Bontsebra)
Equus quagga

Slender Mongoose

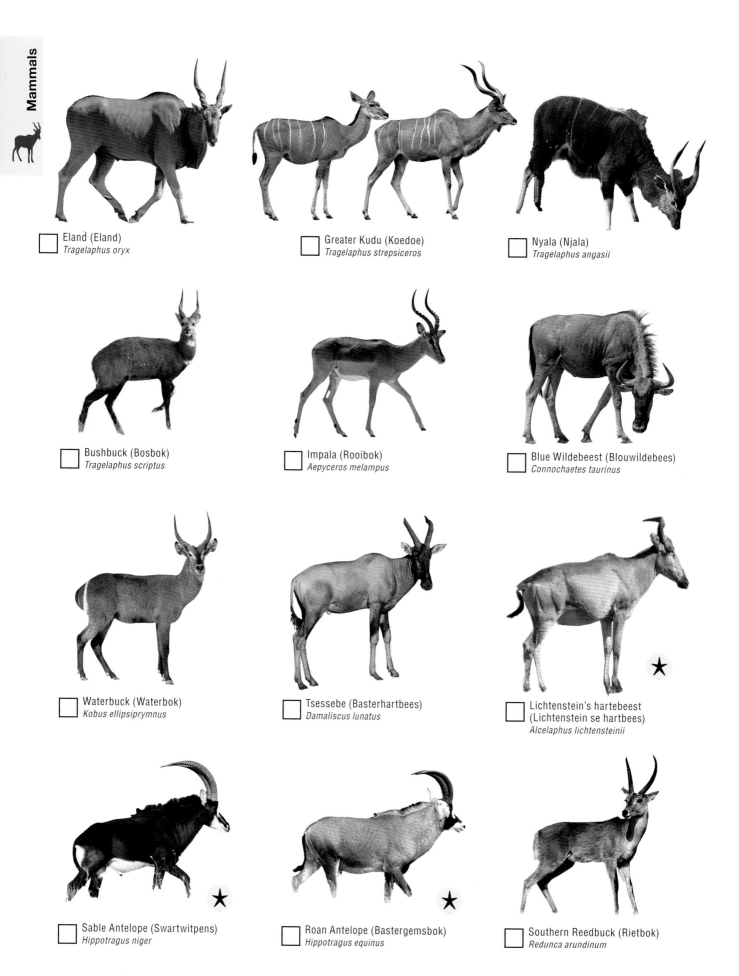

☐ Eland (Eland)
Tragelaphus oryx

☐ Greater Kudu (Koedoe)
Tragelaphus strepsiceros

☐ Nyala (Njala)
Tragelaphus angasii

☐ Bushbuck (Bosbok)
Tragelaphus scriptus

☐ Impala (Rooibok)
Aepyceros melampus

☐ Blue Wildebeest (Blouwildebees)
Connochaetes taurinus

☐ Waterbuck (Waterbok)
Kobus ellipsiprymnus

☐ Tsessebe (Basterhartbees)
Damaliscus lunatus

☐ Lichtenstein's hartebeest
(Lichtenstein se hartbees)
Alcelaphus lichtensteinii ★

☐ Sable Antelope (Swartwitpens)
Hippotragus niger ★

☐ Roan Antelope (Bastergemsbok)
Hippotragus equinus ★

☐ Southern Reedbuck (Rietbok)
Redunca arundinum

☐ Sharpe's Grysbok
(Tropiese Grysbok) ★
Raphicerus sharpei

☐ Klipspringer (Klipspringer)
Oreotragus oreotragus

☐ Steenbok (Steenbok)
Raphicerus campestris

☐ Common or Grey Duiker
(Gewone Duiker)
Sylvicarpa grimmia

☐ Bushpig (Bosvark) ★
Potamochoerus larvatus

☐ Scrub Hare (Kolhaas)
Lepus saxatilis

☐ Ground Pangolin (Ietermagog) ★
Manis temminckii

☐ Common Warthog (Vlakvark)
Phacochoerus africanus

☐ Porcupine (Ystervark)
Hystrix africaeaustralis

☐ Rock Hyrax (Dassie)
Procavia capensis

☐ Tree Squirrel (Boomeekhoring)
Paraxerus cepapi

☐ Springhare (Springhaas)
Pedetes capensis

☐ South African Galago or
Lesser Bushbaby (Nagapie)
Galago moholi

☐ Vervet Monkey (Blouaap)
Cercopithecus pygerythrus

☐ Chacma Baboon (Bobbejaan)
Papio hamadryas

☐ Greater Galago (Bosnagaap)
Otolemur crassicaudatus

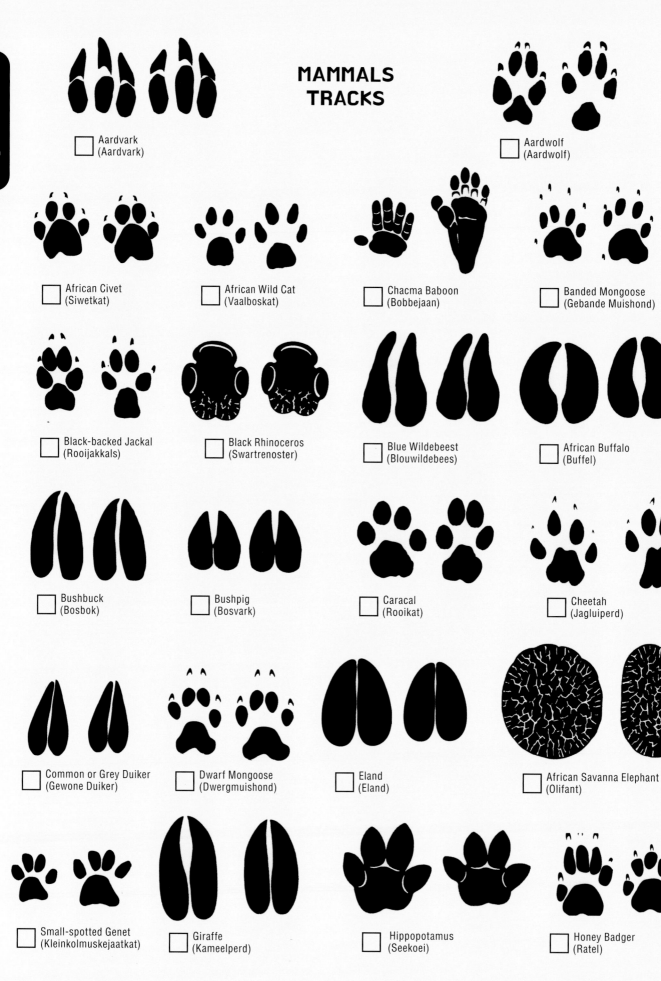

MAMMALS TRACKS

☐ Aardvark
(Aardvark)

☐ Aardwolf
(Aardwolf)

☐ African Civet
(Siwetkat)

☐ African Wild Cat
(Vaalboskat)

☐ Chacma Baboon
(Bobbejaan)

☐ Banded Mongoose
(Gebande Muishond)

☐ Black-backed Jackal
(Rooijakkals)

☐ Black Rhinoceros
(Swartrenoster)

☐ Blue Wildebeest
(Blouwildebees)

☐ African Buffalo
(Buffel)

☐ Bushbuck
(Bosbok)

☐ Bushpig
(Bosvark)

☐ Caracal
(Rooikat)

☐ Cheetah
(Jagluiperd)

☐ Common or Grey Duiker
(Gewone Duiker)

☐ Dwarf Mongoose
(Dwergmuishond)

☐ Eland
(Eland)

☐ African Savanna Elephant
(Olifant)

☐ Small-spotted Genet
(Kleinkolmuskejaatkat)

☐ Giraffe
(Kameelperd)

☐ Hippopotamus
(Seekoei)

☐ Honey Badger
(Ratel)

☐ Honey Badger
(Ratel)

☐ Klipspringer
(Klipspringer)

☐ Greater Kudu
(Koedoe)

☐ Leopard
(Luiperd)

☐ Lion
(Leeu)

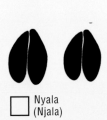
☐ Nyala
(Njala)

☐ Ground Pangolin
(Ietermagog)

☐ Porcupine
(Ystervark)

☐ Southern Reedbuck
(Rietbok)

☐ Roan Antelope
(Bastergemsbok)

☐ Sable Antelope
(Swartwitpens)

☐ Serval
(Tierboskat)

☐ Sharpe's Grysbok
(Tropiese Grysbok)

☐ Side-striped Jackal
(Witkwasjakkals)

☐ Slender Mongoose
(Swartkwasmuishond)

☐ Spotted Hyena
(Gevlekte Hiëna)

☐ Common Warthog
(Vlakvark)

☐ Waterbuck
(Waterbok)

☐ Steenbok
(Steenbok)

☐ Tsessebe
(Basterhartbees)

☐ White Rhinoceros
(Witrenoster)

☐ White-tailed Mongoose
(Witstertmuishond)

☐ African Wild Dog
(Wildehond)

☐ Honey Badger
(Ratel)

REPTILES

Numerous reptile species occur in Kruger, but many are small and seldom seen from a game-drive vehicle.

The reptiles most likely to be spotted may include the Nile crocodile, the largest reptile on Earth, marsh terrapins in pools near rivers, leopard tortoises on the road, rock leguaans in the veld and water leguaans near bodies of water. Snakes do well in savanna and a special sighting would be to see a python. Although several snake species are harmless, there are a few that should be avoided. The black mamba is extremely poisonous, as are cobras and adders. Use a flashlight when walking in the camp at night and look where you are going. Reptiles are fascinating creatures and should be treated with care and respect.

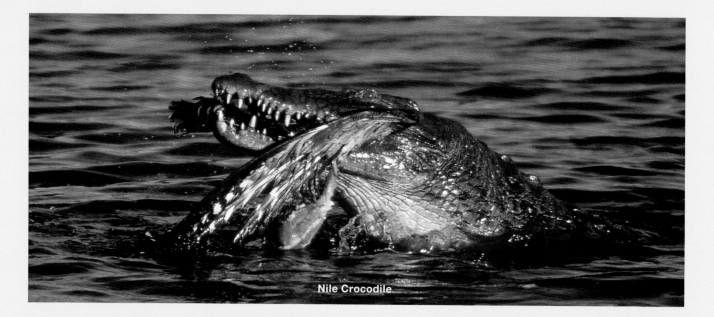
Nile Crocodile

☐ Spotted Bush Snake (Gespikkelde Bosslang)
Philothamnus semivariegatus

☐ Mole Snake (Molslang)
Pseudaspis cana

☐ Boomslang or Tree Snake (Boomslang)
Dispholidus t. typus

☐ Twig Snake (Takslang)
Thelotornis capensis

☐ Snouted Cobra (Egiptiese Kobra)
Naja annulifera

☐ Mozambique Spitting Cobra (Mosambiek Kobra)
Naja mossambica

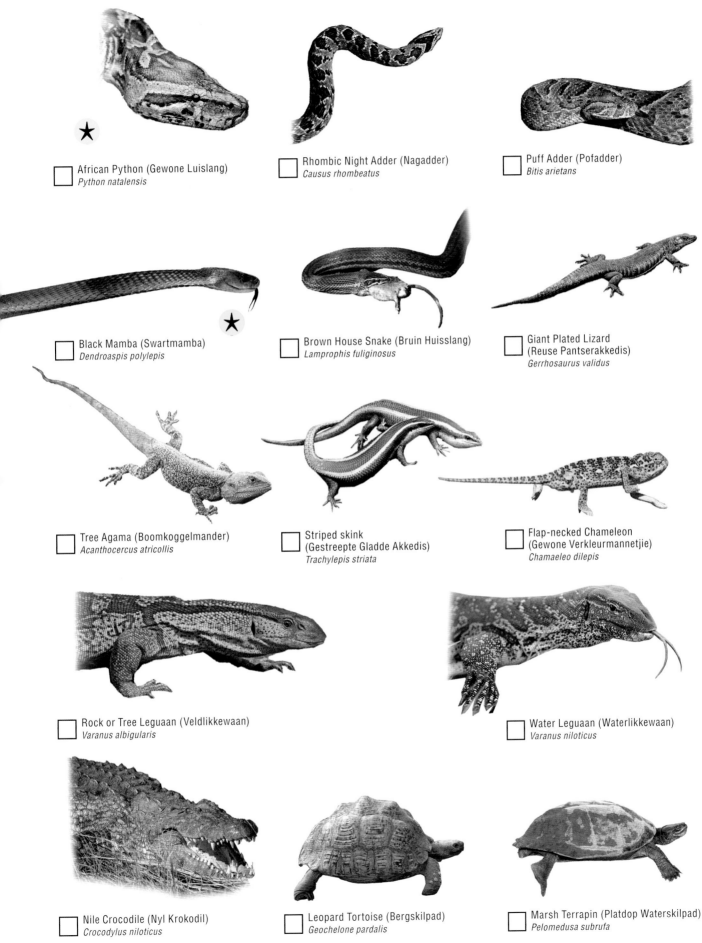

☐ African Python (Gewone Luislang)
Python natalensis
★

☐ Rhombic Night Adder (Nagadder)
Causus rhombeatus

☐ Puff Adder (Pofadder)
Bitis arietans

☐ Black Mamba (Swartmamba)
Dendroaspis polylepis
★

☐ Brown House Snake (Bruin Huisslang)
Lamprophis fuliginosus

☐ Giant Plated Lizard
(Reuse Pantserakkedis)
Gerrhosaurus validus

☐ Tree Agama (Boomkoggelmander)
Acanthocercus atricollis

☐ Striped skink
(Gestreepte Gladde Akkedis)
Trachylepis striata

☐ Flap-necked Chameleon
(Gewone Verkleurmannetjie)
Chamaeleo dilepis

☐ Rock or Tree Leguaan (Veldlikkewaan)
Varanus albigularis

☐ Water Leguaan (Waterlikkewaan)
Varanus niloticus

☐ Nile Crocodile (Nyl Krokodil)
Crocodylus niloticus

☐ Leopard Tortoise (Bergskilpad)
Geochelone pardalis

☐ Marsh Terrapin (Platdop Waterskilpad)
Pelomedusa subrufa

BIRDS

Birding is becoming more popular than ever. Start to notice birds and enrich your game-drive experience. It is surprising how much other game you will see while watching for birds.

There are more than 420 bird species regularly seen in the park; some occasional visitors take the number beyond the 500 mark. For a novice birder it may be difficult to identify any of these. If you are interested in getting started, a visual guide may be useful. Once you can identify the most common birds in the park and a few others, you are on your way to discovering a fascinating new world.

This section shows all birds of the park as thumbnail images.

African Finfoot

☐ Common Ostrich
Volstruis

☐ Crested Guineafowl
Kuifkoptarentaal

☐ Helmeted Guineafowl
Gewone Tarentaal

☐ Harlequin Quail
Bontkwartel

☐ Coqui Francolin
Swempie

☐ Crested Francolin
Bospatrys

☐ Shelley's Francolin
Laeveldpatrys

☐ Greater Flamingo
Grootflamink

☐ Lesser Flamingo
Kleinflamink

☐ Natal Spurfowl
Natalse Fisant

☐ Swainson's Spurfowl
Bosveldfisant

- [ ] Southern Pochard
  Bruineend
- [ ] African Black Duck
  Swarteend
- [ ] Yellow-billed Duck
  Geelbekeend
- [ ] African Pygmy Goose
  Dwerggans

- [ ] Fulvous Whistling Duck
  Fluiteend
- [ ] Knob-billed (Comb) Duck
  Knobbeleend
- [ ] Egyptian Goose
  Kolgans
- [ ] Spur-winged Goose
  Wildemakou

- [ ] White-backed Duck
  Witrugeend
- [ ] White-faced Whistling Duck
  Nonnetjie-eend
- [ ] Hottentot Teal
  Gevlekte Eend
- [ ] Red-billed Teal
  Rooibekeend

- [ ] Little Grebe
  Kleindobbertjie
- [ ] Hamerkop
  Hamerkop
- [ ] African Openbill
  Oopbekooievaar
- [ ] Abdim's Stork
  Kleinswartooievaar

- [ ] Reed Cormorant
  Rietduiker
- [ ] White-breasted Cormorant
  Witborsduiker
- [ ] African Darter
  Slanghalsvoël
- [ ] Marabou Stork
  Maraboe
- [ ] Saddle-billed Stork
  Saalbekooievaar

- [ ] Great White Pelican
  Witpelikaan
- [ ] Black Stork
  Grootswartooievaar
- [ ] Yellow-billed Stork
  Nimmersat
- [ ] White Stork
  Witooievaar
- [ ] Woolly-necked Stork
  Wolnekooievaar

15

Black-crowned Night Heron
Gewone Nagreier ★

Green-backed Heron
Groenrugreier

Squacco Heron
Ralreier

White-backed Night Heron
Witrugnagreier

Purple Heron
Rooireier

Black Heron
Swartreier ★

Goliath Heron
Reusereier

Black-headed Heron
Swartkopreier

Grey Heron
Bloureier

Great Egret
Grootwitreier

Little Egret
Kleinwitreier

Western Cattle Egret
Veereier

Yellow-billed (Intermediate) Egret
Geelbekwitreier

Dwarf Bittern
Dwerggrietreier

Little Bittern
Kleinrietreier

Western Osprey
Visvalk

Shikra
Gebande Sperwer

Hadeda Ibis
Hadeda

Glossy Ibis
Glansibis

African Marsh Harrier
Afrikaanse Vleivalk

Montagu's Harrier
Blouvleivalk

African Sacred Ibis
Skoorsteenveer

African Spoonbill
Lepelaar

Secretarybird
Sekretarisvoël

Pallid Harrier
Witborsvleivalk

☐ African Cuckoo Hawk
Koekoekvalk

☐ African Harrier-Hawk ★
Kaalwangvalk

☐ Dickinson's Kestrel
Dickinsongrysvalk

☐ Bateleur ★
Berghaan

★ ☐ Bat Hawk
Vlermuisvalk

☐ Black Kite
Swartwou

☐ Common (Steppe) Buzzard
Bruinjakkalsvoël

☐ European Honey Buzzard
Wespedief

☐ Black-shouldered Kite
Blouvalk

☐ Yellow-billed Kite
Geelbekwou

☐ Jackal Buzzard
Rooiborsjakkalsvoël

☐ Lizard Buzzard
Akkedisvalk

☐ African Goshawk
Afrikaanse Sperwer

☐ Dark Chanting Goshawk
Donkersingvalk

☐ Black-chested Snake Eagle
Swartborsslangarend

☐ Booted Eagle
Dwergarend

☐ Gabar Goshawk
Witkruissperwer/klein singvalk

★ ☐ African Fish Eagle
Visarend

☐ Brown Snake Eagle
Bruinslangarend

☐ Crowned Eagle
Kroonarend

☐ African Hawk Eagle
Grootjagarend

☐ Ayres's Hawk Eagle
Kleinjagarend

☐ Lesser Spotted Eagle
Gevlekte Arend

☐ Long-crested Eagle
Langkuifarend

☐ Martial Eagle
Breekoparend

☐ Steppe Eagle
Steppe-arend

☐ Little Sparrowhawk
Kleinsperwer

☐ Ovambo Sparrowhawk
Ovambomsperwer

☐ Tawny Eagle
Roofarend

☐ Verreaux's Eagle
Witkruisarend

☐ Red-crested Korhaan
Boskorhaan

☐ Wahlberg's Eagle
Bruinarend

☐ Black Sparrowhawk
Swartsperwer

☐ Black-bellied Bustard
Langbeenkorhaan

☐ Kori Bustard
Gompou

☐ Egyptian Vulture
Egiptiese Aasvoël

☐ Hooded Vulture
Monnikaasvoël

☐ Palm-nut Vulture
Witaasvoël

☐ Common Moorhen
Grootwaterhoender

☐ Lesser Moorhen
Kleinwaterhoender

☐ African Rail
Grootriethaan

☐ Cape Vulture
Kransaasvoël

☐ Lappet-faced Vulture
Swartaasvoël

☐ Red-knobbed Coot
Bleshoender

☐ African Crake
Afrikaanse Riethaan

☐ Black Crake
Swartriethaan

☐ Corn Crake
Kwartelkoning

☐ Striped Crake
Gestreepte Riethaan

☐ Allen's Gallinule
Kleinkoningriethaan

☐ White-headed Vulture
Witkopaasvoël

☐ White-backed Vulture
Witrugaasvoël

☐ African Swamphen
Grootkoningriethaan

☐ Red-chested Flufftail
Rooiborsvleikuiken

☐ African Finfoot
Watertrapper

☐ Spotted Thick-knee
Gewone Dikkop

☐ Water Thick-knee
Waterdikkop

☐ Black-winged Stilt
Rooipootelsie

☐ Senegal Lapwing
Kleinswartvlerkkiewiet

☐ White-crowned Lapwing
Witkopkiewiet

☐ Greater Painted-Snipe
Goudsnip

☐ Pied Avocet
Bontelsie

☐ Caspian Plover
Asiatiese Strandkiewiet

☐ Common Ringed Plover
Ringnekstrandkiewiet

☐ African Jacana
Grootlangtoon

☐ Lesser Jacana
Dwerglangtoon

☐ Ruff
Kemphaan

☐ Kittlitz's Plover
Geelborsstrandkiewiet

☐ Three-banded Plover
Driebandstrandkiewiet

☐ White-fronted Plover
Vaalstrandkiewiet

☐ Common Sandpiper
Gewone Ruiter

☐ Curlew Sandpiper
Krombekstrandloper

☐ Green Sandpiper
Witgatruiter

☐ African Wattled Lapwing
Lelkiewiet

☐ Blacksmith Lapwing
Bontkiewiet

☐ Crowned Lapwing
Kroonkiewiet

☐ Marsh Sandpiper
Moerasruiter

☐ Wood Sandpiper
Bosruiter

☐ Common Greenshank
Groenpootruiter

☐ Little Stint
Kleinstrandloper

☐ African Snipe
Afrikaanse Snip

☐ Kurrichane Buttonquail
Bosveldkwarteltjie

☐ Eurasian Hobby
Europese Boomvalk

☐ Lesser Kestrel
Kleinrooivalk

☐ Rock Kestrel
Kransvalk

☐ Bronze-winged Courser
Bronsvlerkdrawwertjie

☐ Temminck's Courser
Trekdrawwertjie

☐ Three-banded Courser
Driebanddrawwertjie

☐ Amur Falcon
Oostelike Rooipootvalk

☐ Lanner Falcon
Edelvalk

☐ Peregrine Falcon
Swerfvalk

☐ Collared Pratincole
Rooivlerksprinkaanvoël

☐ Grey-headed Gull
Gryskopmeeu

☐ African Skimmer
Waterploeër

☐ Whiskered Tern
Witbaardsterretjie

☐ White-winged Tern
Witvlerksterretjie

☐ Red-footed Falcon
Westelike Rooipootvalk

☐ Sooty Falcon
Roetvalk

☐ Double-banded Sandgrouse
Dubbelbandsandpatrys

19

☐ African Green Pigeon
Papegaaiduif

☐ Speckled Pigeon
Kransduif

☐ African Mourning Dove
Rooioogtortelduif

☐ Brown-headed Parrot
Bruinkoppapegaai

☐ Grey-headed Parrot ★
Savannepapegaai

☐ Cape Turtle-Dove
Gewone Tortelduif

☐ Emerald-spotted Wood-Dove
Groenvlekduifie

☐ Laughing Dove
Rooiborsduifie

☐ Meyer's Parrot
Bosveldpapegaai

☐ Namaqua Dove
Namakwaduifie

☐ Red-eyed Dove
Grootringduif

☐ Tambourine Dove
Witborsduifie

☐ Grey Go-away-bird
Kwêvoël

☐ Purple-crested Turaco ★
Bloukuifloerie

☐ Black Coucal
Swartvleiloerie

☐ Burchell's Coucal
Gewone Vleiloerie

☐ Diederik Cuckoo ★
Diederikkie

☐ Great Spotted Cuckoo
Gevlekte Koekoek

☐ Senegal Coucal
Senegalvleiloerie

☐ African Cuckoo
Afrikaanse Koekoek

☐ Jacobin Cuckoo
Bontnuwejaarsvoël

☐ Klaas's Cuckoo
Meitjie

☐ Levaillant's Cuckoo
Gestreepte Nuwejaarsvoël

☐ Black Cuckoo
Swartkoekoek

☐ Common Cuckoo
Europese Koekoek

☐ Red-chested Cuckoo ★
Piet-My-Vrou

☐ Thick-billed Cuckoo
Dikbekkoekoek

☐ African Grass Owl
Grasuil

☐ African Scops Owl
Skopsuil / Witwanguil

☐ Pearl-spotted Owlet
Witkoluil

☐ African Barred Owlet
Gebande Uil

☐ African Wood Owl
Bosuil

☐ Marsh Owl
Vlei-Uil

☐ Western Barn Owl
Nonnetjie-Uil

☐ Pel's Fishing Owl
Visuil

☐ Southern White-faced Owl
Witwanguil

☐ Verreaux's Eagle-Owl
Reuse-Ooruil

☐ Spotted Eagle-Owl
Gevlekte Ooruil

☐ European Nightjar
Europese Naguil

☐ Fiery-necked Nightjar
Afrikaanse Naguil ♂

☐ Freckled Nightjar
Donkernaguil

☐ Pennant-winged Nightjar
Wimpelvlerknaguil

☐ Rufous-cheeked Nightjar
Rooiwangnaguil

☐ Square-tailed Nightjar
Laeveldnaguil

☐ African Black Swift
Swartwindswael

☐ African Palm Swift
Palmwindswael

☐ Alpine Swift
Witpenswindswael

☐ Common Swift
Europese Windswael

☐ Horus Swift
Horuswindswael

☐ Little Swift
Kleinwindswael

☐ Narina Trogon
Bosloerie

☐ Red-faced Mousebird
Rooiwangmuisvoël

☐ Speckled Mousebird
Gevlekte muisvoël

☐ White-rumped Swift
Witkruiswindswael

☐ Böhm's Spinetail
Witpensstekelstert

☐ Mottled Spinetail
Gevlekte Stekelstert

21

African Pygmy Kingfisher
Dwergvisvanger

Malachite Kingfisher
Kuifkopvisvanger

Half-collared Kingfisher
Blouvisvanger

Blue-cheeked Bee-eater
Blouwangbyvreter

European Bee-eater
Europese Byvreter

Brown-hooded Kingfisher
Bruinkopvisvanger

Grey-headed Kingfisher
Gryskopvisvanger

Giant Kingfisher
Reusevisvanger

Little Bee-eater
Kleinbyvreter

Southern Carmine Bee-eater
Rooiborsbyvreter

Pied Kingfisher
Bontvisvanger

Striped Kingfisher
Gestreepte visvanger

Woodland Kingfisher
Bosveldvisvanger

Swallow-tailed Bee-eater
Swaelstertbyvreter

White-fronted Bee-eater
Rooikeelbyvreter

Broad-billed Roller
Geelbektroupant

European Roller
Europese Troupant

Lilac-breasted Roller
Gewone Troupant

African Grey Hornbill
Grysneushoringvoël

Crowned Hornbill
Gekroonde Neushoringvoël

Purple Roller
Groottroupant

Racket-tailed Roller
Knopsterttroupant

Green Wood-Hoopoe
Rooibekkakelaar

Southern Yellow-billed Hornbill
Geelbekneushoringvoël

Southern Red-billed Hornbill
Rooibekneushoringvoël

African Hoopoe
Hoephoep

Common Scimitarbill
Swartbekkakelaar

Trumpeter Hornbill
Gewone Boskraai

Southern Ground-Hornbill
Bromvoël

☐ Bearded Woodpecker
Baardspeg

☐ Bennett's Woodpecker
Bennettspeg

☐ Chestnut-backed Sparrowlark
Rooiruglewerik

☐ Dusky Lark
Donkerlewerik

☐ Cardinal Woodpecker
Kardinaalspeg

☐ Golden-tailed Woodpecker
Goudstertspeg

☐ Fawn-coloured Lark
Vaalbruinlewerik

☐ Flappet Lark
Laeveldklappertjie

☐ Greater Honeyguide
Grootheuningwyser

☐ Grey-backed Sparrowlark
Grysruglewerik

☐ Monotonous Lark
Bosveldlewerik

☐ Red-capped Lark
Rooikoplewerik

☐ Lesser Honeyguide
Kleinheuningwyser

☐ Scaly-throated Honeyguide
Gevlekte Heuningwyser

☐ Brown-backed Honeybird
Skerpbekheuningvoël

☐ Rufous-naped Lark
Rooineklewerik

☐ Sabota Lark
Sabotalewerik

☐ Bushveld Pipit
Bosveldkoester

☐ Black Saw-wing
Swartsaagvlerkswael

☐ Brown-throated Martin
Afrikaanse Oewerswael

☐ Common House-Martin
Huisswael

☐ Wire-tailed Swallow
Draadstertswael

☐ African Pied Wagtail
Bontkwikkie

☐ Cape Wagtail
Gewone Kwikkie

☐ Rock Martin
Kransswael

☐ Sand Martin
Europese Oewerswael

☐ Barn Swallow
Europese Swael

☐ Mountain Wagtail
Bergkwikkie

☐ Western Yellow Wagtail
Geelkwikkie

☐ Yellow-throated Longclaw
Geelkeelkalkoentjie

☐ Grey-rumped Swallow
Gryskruisswael

☐ Lesser Striped Swallow
Kleinstreepswael

☐ Mosque Swallow
Moskeeswael

☐ Plain-backed Pipit
Donkerkoester

☐ Striped Pipit
Gestreepte Koester

☐ African Pipit
Gewone Koester

☐ Pearl-breasted Swallow
Perelborsswael

☐ Red-breasted Swallow
Rooiborsswael

☐ White-throated Swallow
Witkeelswael

☐ Buffy Pipit
Vaalkoester

☐ Black Cuckooshrike
Swartkatakoeroe

☐ White-breasted Cuckooshrike
Witborskatakoeroe

Terrestrial
Brownbul
Boskrapper

Dark-capped
Bulbul
Swartoogtiptol

Sombre Greenbul
Gewone Willie

Croaking Cisticola
Groot Tinktinkie

Desert Cisticola
Woestynklopkloppie

Lazy Cisticola
Luitinktinkie

Yellow-bellied
Greenbul
Geelborswillie

Willow Warbler
Hofsanger

Stierling's
Wren-Warbler
Stierlingsanger

Rattling Cisticola
Bosveldtinktinkie

Red-faced Cisticola
Rooiwangtinktinkie

Rufous-winged
Cisticola
Swartrugtinktinkie

Burnt-necked
Eremomela
Buinkeelbossanger

Green-capped
Eremomela
Donkerwangbossanger

Yellow-bellied
Eremomela
Geelpensbossanger

Zitting Cisticola
Landeryklopkloppie

Green-backed
Camaroptera
Groenrugkwekwevoël

Grey-backed
Camaroptera
Grysrugkwekwevoël

Bar-throated Apalis
Bandkeel-kleinjantjie

Rudd's Apalis
Ruddkleinjantjie

Yellow-breasted
Apalis
Geelborskleinjantjie

Neddicky
Neddikkie

Tawny-flanked
Prinia
Bruinsylangstertjie

Long-billed
Crombec
Bosveldstompstert

African Reed
Warbler
Kleinrietsanger

Broad-tailed
Warbler
Breëstertsanger

Dark-capped
Yellow Warbler
Geelsanger

Southern Hyliota
Mashonahyliota

Common
Whitethroat
Witkeelsanger

Chestnut-vented
Tit-Babbler
Bosveldtjeriktik

Garden Warbler
Tuinsanger

Great Reed Warbler
Grootrietsanger

Icterine Warbler
Spotsanger

Collared
Palm-Thrush
Palmmorelyster

Groundscraper
Thrush
Gevlekte Lyster

Kurrichane Thrush
Rooibeklyster

Lesser
Swamp Warbler
Kaapse Rietsanger

Little Rush Warbler
Kaapse vleisanger

Marsh Warbler
Europese Rietsanger

Capped Wheatear
Hoëveldskaapwagter

African Stonechat
Gewone Bontrokkie

Cape Robin-Chat
Gewone Janfrederik

Olive-tree Warbler
Olyfboomsanger

River Warbler
Sprinkaansanger

Sedge Warbler
Europese Vleisanger

Red-capped
Robin-Chat
Nataljanfrederik

White-browed
Robin-Chat
Heuglinjanfrederik

White-throated
Robin-Chat
Witkeeljanfrederik

Bearded Scrub Robin
Baardwipstert

White-browed Scrub Robin
Gestreepte Wipstert

Thrush Nightingale
Lysternagtegaal

Southern Black Flycatcher
Swartvlieëvanger

Spotted Flycatcher
Europese Vlieëvanger

Cape Batis
Kaapse Bosbontrokkie

Arnot's Chat
Bontpiek

Familiar Chat
Gewone Spekvreter

Mocking Cliff Chat
Dassievoël

Chinspot Batis
Witliesbosbontrokkie

Black-throated Wattle-eye
Beloogbosbontrokkie

African Paradise Flycatcher
Paradysvlieëvanger

Ashy Flycatcher
Blougrysvlieëvanger

African Dusky Flycatcher
Donkervlieëvanger

Fiscal Flycatcher
Fiskaalvlieëvanger

Blue-mantled Crested-Flycatcher
Bloukuifvlieëvanger

Arrow-marked Babbler
Pylvlekkatlagter

Crested Barbet
Kuifkophoutkapper

Grey Tit-Flycatcher
Waaierstertvlieëvanger

Marico Flycatcher
Maricovlieëvanger

Pale Flycatcher
Muiskleurvlieëvanger

Acacia Pied Barbet
Bonthoutkapper

Black-collared Barbet
Rooikophoutkapper

Yellow-fronted Tinkerbird
Geelblestinker

Yellow-rumped Tinkerbird
Swartblestinker

Amethyst Sunbird
Swartsuikerbekkie

Collared Sunbird
Kortbeksuikerbekkie

Eastern Nicator
Geelvleknikator

African Golden Oriole
Afrikaanse Wielewaal

Black-headed Oriole
Swartkopwielewaal

Marico Sunbird
Maricosuikerbekkie

Purple-banded Sunbird
Purperbandsuikerbekkie

Scarlet-chested Sunbird
Rooiborssuikerbekkie

Eurasian Golden Oriole
Europese Wielewaal

Crimson-breasted Shrike
Rooiborslaksman

Lesser Grey Shrike
Gryslaksman

White-bellied Sunbird
Witpenssuikerbekkie

African Yellow White-eye
Geelglasogie

Cape White-eye
Kaapse Glasogie

Magpie Shrike
Langstertlaksman

Red-backed Shrike
Rooiruglaksman

Southern Black Tit
Gewone Swartmees

Grey Penduline Tit
Gryskapokvoël

Tropical Boubou
Tropiese Waterfiskaal

Southern White-crowned Shrike
Kremetartlaksman

Southern (Common) Fiscal
Fiskaallaksman

Fork-tailed Drongo
Mikstertbyvanger

25

☐ Southern Boubou
Suidelike Waterfiskaal

☐ Brubru
Bontroklaksman

☐ Red-billed Oxpecker
Rooibekrenostervoël

☐ Yellow-billed Oxpecker
Geelbekrenostervoël

☐ Common Myna
Indiese Spreeu

☐ Gorgeous Bush-Shrike
Konkoit

☐ Grey-headed Bush-Shrike
Spookvoël

☐ Olive Bush-Shrike
Olyfboslaksman

☐ Pied Crow
Witborskraai

☐ Black-bellied Starling
Swartpensglansspreeu

☐ Burchell's Starling
Grootglansspreeu

☐ Orange-breasted Bush-Shrike
Oranjeborsboslaksman

☐ Black-backed Puffback
Sneeubal

☐ Black-crowned Tchagra
Swaartkroontjagra

☐ Cape Glossy Starling
Kleinglansspreeu

☐ Greater Blue-eared Starling
Grootblouoorglansspreeu

☐ Meves's Starling
Langstertglansspreeu

☐ Brown-crowned Tchagra
Rooivlerktjagra

☐ Retz's Helmet-Shrike
Swarthelmlaksman

☐ White-crested Helmet-Shrike
Withelmlaksman

☐ Red-winged Starling
Rooivlerkspreeu

☐ Violet-backed Starling
Witborsspreeu

☐ Wattled Starling
Lelspreeu

☐ White-browed Sparrow-Weaver
Koringvoël

☐ African (Holub's) Golden Weaver
Goudwewer

☐ Lesser Masked-Weaver
Kleingeelvink

☐ Fan-tailed Widowbird
Kortstertflap

☐ Red-collared Widowbird
Rooikeelflap

☐ White-winged Widowbird
Witvlerkflap

☐ Red-billed Buffalo Weaver
Buffelwewer

☐ Red-headed Weaver
Rooikopwewer

☐ Southern Brown-throated Weaver
Bruinkeelwewer

☐ Red-billed Quelea
Rooibekkwelea

☐ Southern Red Bishop
Rooivink

☐ Yellow-crowned Bishop
Goudgeelvink

☐ Southern Masked Weaver
Swartkeelgeelvink

☐ Spectacled Weaver
Brilwewer

☐ Thick-billed Weaver
Dikbekwewer

☐ Cuckoo Finch
Koekoekvink

☐ Village Weaver
Bontrugwewer

☐ Yellow Weaver
Kaapse wewer / Geelwewer

Cut-throat Finch
Bandkeelvink

Red-headed Finch
Rooikopvink

African Firefinch
Kaapse Vuurvinkie

Jameson's Firefinch
Jamesonvuurvinkie

Red-billed Firefinch
Rooibekvuurvinkie

Green-winged Pytilia
Gewone Melba

Orange-winged Pytilia
Oranjevlerkmelba

African Quail-finch
Gewone Kwartelvinkie

Bronze Mannikin
Gewone Fret

Red-backed Mannikin
Rooirugfret

Green Twinspot
Groenkolpensie

Long-tailed Paradise-Whydah
Gewone Paradysvink

Shaft-tailed Whydah
Pylstertrooibekkie

Pin-tailed Whydah
Koningrooibekkie

Pink-throated Twinspot
Rooskeelkolpensie

Blue Waxbill
Gewone Blousysie

Common Waxbill
Rooibeksysie

Dusky Indigobird
Gewone Blouvinkie

Purple Indigobird
Witpootblouvinkie

Village Indigobird
Staalblouvinkie

Orange-breasted Waxbill
Rooiassie

Violet-eared Waxbill
Koningblousysie

Cinnamon-breasted Bunting
Klipstreepkoppie

Golden-breasted Bunting
Rooirugstreepkoppie

Lark-like Bunting
Vaalstreepkoppie

Brimstone Canary
Dikbekkanarie

Lemon-breasted Canary
Geelborskanarie

Yellow-fronted Canary
Geeloogkanarie

Streaky-headed Seedeater
Streepkopkanarie

Yellow-throated Petronia
Geelvlekmossie

Cape Sparrow
Gewone mossie

House Sparrow
Huismossie

Southern Grey-headed Sparrow
Gryskopmossie

TREES

Tree spotting is an entertaining activity on game drives. Trees give so many clues about geology, animals and the entire web of life that they simply cannot be ignored. Start with a tree-spotting activity and be surprised how revealing and satisfying it becomes.

South Africa is home to an astounding diversity of tree species; 1 300 are indigenous and 336 of these occur in the Kruger National Park. This means the park has an indigenous tree diversity that equals 25% of all the species occurring in South Africa and three times more than those indigenous to the whole of Europe. Even more astonishing is that the park covers only about 2.5% of the surface area of South Africa.

The Kruger National Park is about the size of Wales or Israel, yet it has a tremendous botanical diversity. Plant diversity goes hand in hand with geographical diversity since geology, soil types, topography, climate and rainfall are all interlinked. All this helps to define different landscapes and ecozones. This in turn influences the plant feeders, and the presence of plant feeders influences the occurrence of predators.

Even though the park's geology is fairly simple, its landscapes are quite varied and diverse.

Baobab Flower

☐ Red Bushwillow (Rooiboswilg)
Combretum apiculatum

☐ Russet Bushwillow (Kierieklapper)
Combretum hereroense

☐ Large Fruit Bushwillow (Raasblaar)
Combretum zeyheri

☐ Leadwood (Hardekool)
Combretum imberbe

☐ Marula (Maroela)
Sclerocarya birrea

☐ Bushveld Apple-leaf (Appelblaar)
Philenoptera violacea

☐ Knob-thorn (Knoppiesdoring)
Senegalia (formerly Acacia) nigrescens

☐ Delagoa Thorn (Delagoadoring)
Senegalia (formerly Acacia) welwitschii subsp delagoensis

☐ River Thorn (Brakdoring)
Vachellia (formerly Acacia) robusta

☐ Horned Thorn (Horingdoring)
Vachellia (formerly Acacia) grandicornuta

☐ Umbrella Thorn (Haak-en-steek)
Vachellia (formerly Acacia) tortilis

☐ Fever Tree (Koorsboom)
Vachellia (formerly Acacia) xanthophloea

☐ Greenthorn Torchwood (Groendoring)
Balanites maughamii

☐ Small-leafed Sickle-bush (Sekelbos)
Dichrostachys cinerea subsp. africana

☐ Silver Cluster-leaf (Vaalboom)
Terminalia sericea

☐ Purple-pod Cluster-leaf (Sterkbos)
Terminalia prunioides

☐ Cape Date Palm (Wildedadelpalm)
Phoenix reclinata

☐ Lala Palm (Lalapalm)
Hyphaene coriacea

☐ Bushveld Gardenia (Bosveldkatjiepiering)
Gardenia volkensii

☐ Sycomore Fig (Sycomorusvy)
Ficus sycomorus

☐ Large-leafed Rock Fig (Grootblaarrotsvy)
Ficus abutilifolia

☐ Tamboti (Tambotie)
Spirostachys africana

☐ African Weeping Wattle (Huilboom)
Peltoforum africanum

☐ Many-stemmed Albizia (Meerstamvalsdoring)
Albizia petersiana subsp. evansii

 ★
☐ Baobab (Kremetartboom)
Adansonia digitata

☐ Nyala Tree (Njalaboom)
Xanthocercis zambesiaca

☐ Ebony Jackalberry (Jakalsbessie)
Diospyros mespiliformis

☐ Weeping Boer-bean (Huilboerboon)
Schotia brachypetala

☐ Sausage Tee (Worsboom)
Kigelia africana

☐ Pod Mahogany (Peul-mahonie)
Afzelia quanzensis

☐ Bushveld Natal-Mahogany (Rooiessenhout)
Trichilia emetica

☐ Tree Wisteria (Vanwykshout)
Bolusanthus speciosus

☐ Mopane leaves and flowers (Mopanie)
Colophospermum mopane

☐ Long-tail Cassia (Sambokpeul)
Cassia abbreviata

☐ Round-leafed Bloodwood (Dopperkiaat)
Pterocarpus rotundifolius

 ★
☐ Impala Lily (Impalalelie)
Adenium multiflorum

Red-knobbed Coot

Copyright © 2023 by **HPH Publishing**
First Edition
ISBN 978-1-77632-334-0
Text by Ingrid van den Berg
Photography by Philip & Ingrid van den Berg,
Heinrich van den Berg
Publisher: Heinrich van den Berg
Edited by John Deane
Proofread by Margy Gibson
Design, typesetting and reproduction by
Heinrich van den Berg, **HPH Publishing**
and Nicky Wenhold

All rights reserved. No part of this publication may be
reproduced or transmitted in any form or by any means
without prior written permission from the publisher.
First edition, first impression 2023
Published by **HPH Publishing**
50A, Sixth Street, Linden, 2195, South Africa
info@hphpublishing.co.za, www.hphpublishing.co.za